What Families Do

Katie Peters

GRL Consultant Diane Craig,
Certified Literacy Specialist

Pull Ahead Readers

Lerner Publications ◆ Minneapolis

Note from a GRL Consultant
This Pull Ahead leveled book has been carefully designed for beginning readers. A team of guided reading literacy experts has reviewed and leveled the book to ensure readers pull ahead and experience success.

Lerner Publications
An imprint of Lerner Publishing Group, Inc.
241 First Avenue North
Minneapolis, MN 55401 USA

For reading levels and more information, look up this title at www.lernerbooks.com.

Main body text set in Memphis Pro 24/39
Typeface provided by Linotype.

Photo Acknowledgments
The images in this book are used with the permission of: © StockImageFactory.com/Shutterstock, p. 3; © fizkes/Shutterstock, pp. 4–5, 16 (left); © Drazen Zigic/Shutterstock, pp. 6–7; © PeopleImages.com - Yuri A/Shutterstock, pp. 8–9, 14–15, 16 (middle, right); © Monkey Business Images/Shutterstock, pp. 10–11; © Pressmaster/Shutterstock, pp. 12–13.

Front cover: © People Image Studio/Shutterstock

Library of Congress Cataloging-in-Publication Data

Names: Peters, Katie, author.
Title: What families do / written by Katie Peters.
Description: Minneapolis : Lerner Publications, [2026] | Series: Let's look at families | Includes index. | Audience: Ages 4–7 | Audience: Grades K–1 | Summary: "Reading, walking, and shopping are all things that families do together. Easy-to-read text and colorful photographs show young readers what families do. Pairs with the fiction story, Leo Helps His Family"—Provided by publisher.
Identifiers: LCCN 2025010820 (print) | LCCN 2025010821 (ebook) | ISBN 9798765689844 (library binding) | ISBN 9798348028565 (paperback) | ISBN 9798765695029 (epub)
Subjects: LCSH: Families—Juvenile literature.
Classification: LCC HQ744 .P398 2026 (print) | LCC HQ744 (ebook) | DDC 306.85—dc23/eng/20250512

LC record available at https://lccn.loc.gov/2025010820
LC ebook record available at https://lccn.loc.gov/2025010821

Manufactured in the United States of America
1 – CG – 12/15/25

Table of Contents

What Families Do

We play together.

We shop together.

will she learn how
swim?

We read together.

We walk together.

We eat together.

We are a family.

Did You See It?

blocks

book

bubbles

Index